AF348503

Saved by the Lamb

Moses and Jesus

Saved by the Lamb

Moses and Jesus

Maura Roan McKeegan

Illustrated by T. Schluenderfritz

EMMAUS ROAD
PUBLISHING

Steubenville, Ohio
www.emmausroad.org

Emmaus Road Publishing
1468 Parkview Circle
Steubenville, Ohio 43952

ISBN: 978-1-64585-110-3
Library of Congress Control Number: 2021931668

Design and Illustrations by:
T. Schluenderfritz

Nihil Obstat: Rev. James M. Dunfee, Censor Librorum
March 26, 2019

Imprimatur: Jeffrey M. Monforton, Bishop of Steubenville
March 26, 2019

The nihil obstat and imprimatur are declarations that work is considered to be free from doctrinal or moral error. It is not implied that those who have granted the same agree with the content, opinions, or statements expressed.

Saved by the Lamb

Moses and Jesus

Maura Roan McKeegan

Illustrated by T. Schluenderfritz

Have you heard of a man named Moses?
Do you know about Jesus, too?
One is from the Old Testament,
One is from the New.
Both stories are the Word of God,
Their messages are true;
But when you see them side by side,
A hidden part comes through.

Now take a closer look
At how their histories are told:
See the Holy Spirit work
As mysteries unfold.
Find the buried treasures
That the Sacred Scriptures hold;
Let the New unlock the door
To secrets of the Old!

"The New Testament lies hidden in the Old, and the Old is unveiled in the New."
—Saint Augustine

Long ago, in Egypt,
A baby boy was born.
The baby's Hebrew mother
Lived far away from her people's native land of Israel.
She laid her tiny son in a basket among the reeds at the river's bank,
Because she could not keep him at home.

Long ago, in Bethlehem,
A baby boy was born.
The baby's Hebrew mother
Had traveled far away from her home in Nazareth.
She laid her tiny son in a manger filled with straw,
Because there was no room for them at the inn.

The leader of Egypt, called Pharaoh,
Was trying to kill all the Hebrew baby boys.
But God had a special plan for the child in the basket.
He protected this baby boy
Who grew up in Egypt.
His name was Moses,
And God chose him to lead His people to freedom.

The king of Judea, called Herod,
Was trying to kill all the Hebrew baby boys.
But God had a special plan for the child in the manger.
He protected this baby boy
By sending his family to Egypt.
His name was Jesus,
And He was born to set God's people free.

Moses grew up
And saw the troubles of the people of Israel.
His people, God's chosen people, were slaves.
They were slaves to the Egyptians.
Moses wanted to help them.
One day, Moses was leading a flock of sheep to graze
On a mountain called Horeb,
When the angel of the Lord appeared in a burning bush, a flame of fire,
And God spoke.
He said He was the God of Moses' father.
God was calling Moses to lead the people of Israel
Out of Egypt
To freedom.

Jesus grew up
And saw the troubles of the people of Israel.
His people, God's chosen people, were slaves.
They were slaves to sin.
Jesus wanted to heal them.
One day, Jesus, the Good Shepherd,
Was being baptized in the Jordan River,
When the heavens opened and the Spirit appeared as a dove,
And God spoke.
He said Jesus was His beloved Son.
God had sent Jesus to lead His people
Out of sin
To freedom.

When God's chosen people, the Israelites, were in danger,
He sent Moses to tell them
To sacrifice a lamb.
If they ate its flesh
Along with unleavened bread,
And covered their doorposts with its blood,
The sacrifice of the lamb
Would guard them from the plague of death,
And the people of Israel would be saved.

When God's people were in danger,
God sent Jesus to save them.
Jesus was the Lamb of God.
He would give them His flesh to eat
In the form of unleavened bread,
And His blood to drink.
The sacrifice of Jesus, the Lamb,
Would conquer death,
And God's people would be saved.

Moses led his people
Through the waters of the Red Sea
To a new life.
They stayed in the wilderness for forty years.
Moses told the Israelites to obey God.
When they were hungry,
God sent them heavenly bread,
Called manna, to sustain them.

Jesus led His people
Through the waters of Baptism
To new life.
He fasted in the wilderness for forty days.
Jesus told His people to believe in Him
And they would never be hungry.
He gave them the Bread of Heaven,
The Eucharist, to sustain them.

In the wilderness, the Israelites grumbled and complained,
Even though the Lord took care of them again and again.
God said their hearts were hardened.
When the people were thirsty,
The Lord told Moses to strike a rock,
And water would flow from it for the people to drink.

The scribes and Pharisees complained about Jesus,
Even though He performed miracles to feed and heal the people.
Their hearts were hardened against Him.
Jesus said, "If any one thirst, let him come to me and drink.
He who believes in me, as the Scripture has said,
'Out of his heart shall flow rivers of living water.'"

On a mountain called Sinai,
Moses talked with God.
The Lord called to Moses
Out of the midst of a cloud.
The people of Israel were afraid
Because the skin of Moses' face shone
So brightly that he had to put on a veil
After he had been talking with God.

On a mountain called Tabor,
Jesus' friends saw Him talking with Moses.
They heard God's voice coming from
A bright cloud.
They fell on their faces in awe.
Jesus' face shone like the sun,
And His garments became white as light,
And the disciples saw the glory of God.

A plague of fiery serpents came.
They bit the Israelites, and many people died.
God told Moses
To make a bronze serpent
And mount it on a pole.
If a serpent bit any man,
He would look at the bronze serpent
And live.

A plague of sin
Was leading God's people into death.
God sent Jesus
To become a man
And be lifted up on the Cross.
If sin poisoned any man,
He could believe in Jesus
And have eternal life.

In Egypt, the Israelites had put lamb's blood from a basin onto bunches of hyssop
And lifted the branches to their doorposts and lintels
To cover them with the blood of the lamb,
To preserve the people from death.

On Calvary, soldiers put vinegar from a bowl onto a hyssop branch
And raised it toward the beams of the Cross
To give it to the Lamb of God,
Before He died.

An enemy called Amalek and his men
Attacked the Israelites.
Moses stood on top of a hill
And held up his hands.
His arms got tired,
But whenever he put down his hands,
The enemy prevailed.
So a friend stood on either side of him
And helped to hold up his hands
Until the sun went down,
And the enemy was defeated.
Israel had won the battle!

The enemy, Satan,
Was attacking God's people.
Jesus was nailed to a Cross on top of a hill,
With His arms outstretched.
He was in agony,
But He would not come down from the Cross
And let the enemy prevail.
A thief hung on either side of Him.
His arms were open wide
Until His body was taken down.
The enemy was defeated.
Christ had won the victory!

On Mt. Nebo,
God showed Moses the
Promised Land—Canaan.
Moses led the Israelites there,
But sadly, he died
Before he could enter Canaan.
He would not live on the earth
In the place that the Lord had prepared
For His chosen people.
But God would not forget His servant.
One day, Moses would see the glory of God.

On Mt. Calvary,
Jesus opened the gates to the
Promised Land—heaven.
Jesus led His people there,
And He rose from the dead
So that they could enter heaven.
Now He could bring them to live forever
In the place He promised to prepare
For His beloved children.
God had remembered His people.
Now they could rest in His glory.

You've heard the ancient echo
    Of the Old within the New.
You've looked through the Bible's window
And discovered a hidden view.

As you listen to stories from Scripture
And find wonder in all God can do,
Remember, dear child, that this divine plan
Shows the depth of His great love for you.

Maura Roan McKeegan first learned about biblical typology when she was a graduate student in theology. As a school teacher, she believed that children would be as fascinated by the connections between the Old and New Testaments as she was— and that once they had the key, children could unlock countless hidden treasures in Scripture. This belief inspired her to write the Old and New series of picture books, including the award-winning *The End of the Fiery Sword: Adam & Eve and Jesus & Mary* and *Into the Sea, Out of the Tomb: Jonah & Jesus*. She lives in Ohio with her husband, Shaun, and their four children.

Ted Schluenderfritz is the illustrator of several books including *The Attic Saint, Portrait of the Son,* and *A Life of Our Lord for Children*. He is a freelance graphic designer and the art director for *Gilbert Magazine* and *Living Faith Kids*. He lives in Littleton, Colorado with his wife, Rachel, and their children. You can view more of his work at www.5sparrows.com and @schluenderfritz on Instagram.

More from the Old and New Series

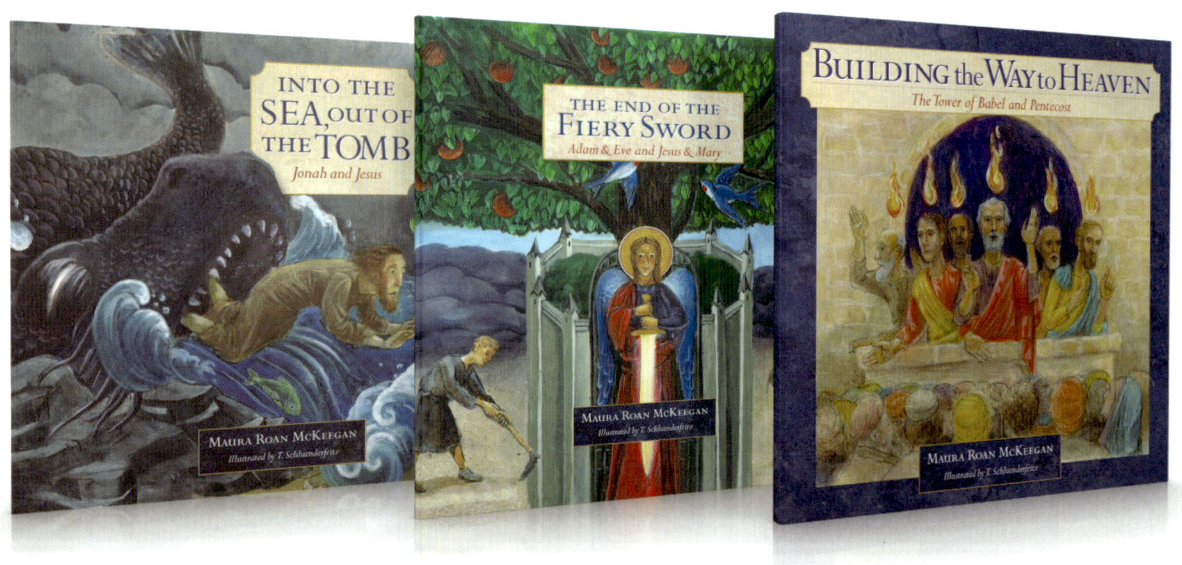